GLORIOUS ANGELS
Coloring Book

JOHN GREEN

Dover Publications, Inc.
Mineola, New York

NOTE

Angels—benevolent spirits that act as guardians and protectors of mortals—have long been a favorite theme in art. Here in this beautiful coloring book noted artist John Green has created thirty illustrations featuring a wide variety of angels. You will find angels from myth and legend and some from the Old and New Testaments as well. Several of the illustrations depict actual Biblical scenes while others show the angels in all their divine glory.

Copyright

Copyright © 2013 by Dover Publications, Inc.
All rights reserved.

Bibliographical Note

Glorious Angels Coloring Book is a new work, first published by
Dover Publications, Inc., in 2012.

International Standard Book Number

ISBN-13: 978-0-486-48046-6
ISBN-10: 0-486-48046-1

Manufactured in the United States by RR Donnelley
48046105   2016
www.doverpublications.com

Achaiah, Angel of Patience

Caracasa, Angel of Spring

Lailah, Angel of the Night

Ramiel, Angel of Thunder

Chermes, Angel of the Ninth Hour of the Night

Cupid, the God of Love

Jacob Wrestling with the Angel

The Archangel Michael

Afriel, a Guardian Angel

Israfel, Angel of Music

Balaam and the Angel

The Archangel Gabriel Appearing Before the Virgin Mary

The Archangel Metatron

Anfial, Angel of Childbirth

Sleeping Angel

Christmas Angel

The Archangel Jophiel

Cherub

Amalek, Angel of the Moon

The Angel Ambriel

The Angel at Jesus's Tomb

The Sacrifice of Isaac by Abraham

The Angel Anahita

Armaita, Angel of Truth

Cathelel, Angel of the Garden

Eloa, Angel of Compassion

Cherubs

The Archangel Raphael and Tobias

Armatt, Angel of Peace

Uriel, Angel of Light